Kiwi

A Children's Devotional

Building Character from the Inside Out

Written by:
Sid A. Taylor, Sr., MSW, M.Div., M.A.C.E., D.Min
Rita Taylor Stewart, M.Ed., M.A.C.E.

Illustrated by:
Charles Ettinger

Faithful Life Publishers
North Fort Myers, FL 33903

FaithfulLifePublishers.com

Kiwi: A Children's Devotional

Copyright © 2012 Sid Taylor, Sr. and Rita T. Stewart

ISBN: 978-1-937129-41-5

Authors: Sid Taylor, Sr. and Rita T. Stewart

Illustrator: Charles Ettinger

Published and printed by:
Faithful Life Publishers
3335 Galaxy Way
North Fort Myers, FL 33903

www.FaithfulLifePublishers.com
info@FLPublishers.com
888.720.0950

Bible translation used: New International Version

All rights reserved. The contents herein may not represent the views of Faithful Life Publishers. No part of this publication may be reproduced, stored in a retrieval system, or transmitted in any form or by any means—electronic, mechanical, photocopy, recording, or any other—without the permission of Sid Taylor, Sr or Rita T. Stewart, and/or Faithful Life Publishers.

Printed in the United States of America.

18 17 16 15 14 13 12   1 2 3 4 5

ACKNOWLEDGEMENTS

Over the years, the Lord has led us to life changing stories that challenged and developed our faith. We are now privileged to contribute to the wealth of knowledge available in the village of faith.

We are grateful to the Holy Spirit and to the writers who have gone before us. We also thank the teachers, preachers, and mentors who have groomed and pruned us. We are, "paying it forward."

Lastly, we want to express deep love and gratitude to our family for their selfless support and as a result this project is now birthed.

It is our prayer that these stories will bless the children by making God real and reachable.

ABOUT THE AUTHORS

For the past 18 years, Sid has served as a U.S. Army Chaplain. He enjoys storytelling, preaching, coffee, and good music. Sid is currently the Deputy Garrison Chaplain at Ft. Meade, Md.

Rita serves as a Christian Educator, Spiritual Director and Gratitude Coach. She enjoys reading, teaching, tea, and traveling with her husband Gerald and daughter Lauren.

DEDICATION

For the children of the world.
We pray that these stories help you to make sense of life
and guide you toward our loving God.

INTRODUCTION

These stories have been inspired by the Holy Spirit
and by all good stories past and present
(parables, fables, and reflections on life). We hope to assist parents and teachers
in their efforts to rear godly children and great citizens of the world.
Our hope is that adults will read these stories to children,
so that the children can ask questions and gain clarity and understanding.

May the children grow to value the following words from the Bible.

*My son, keep your father's commands and do not forsake your mother's teaching.
Bind them upon your heart forever; fasten them around your neck.
When you walk, they will guide you; when you sleep, they will watch over you;
When you awake, they will speak to you. For these commands are a lamp,
this teaching is a light, and the corrections of discipline are the way of life.*
                                        Proverbs 6:20-23

*I will instruct you and teach you in the way you should go;
I will counsel you and watch over you.*
                                        Psalm 32:8

TABLE OF CONTENTS

1. The Golden Rule: Five Dollar Bill 6
2. Obedience: Stop! In the Name of Love 8
3. Gratitude: The Thankful Turkey 10
4. Forgiveness: I Forgot 12
5. Hospitality: Sleepover 14
6. Thrifty: Grab Bag 16
7. Teamwork: 1,2,3, Lift! 18
8. Simplicity: Game Rules 20
9. Doing a Good Job: The Paper Route 22
10. Prayer: Straight Paths 24
11. Diligence: Practice, Practice, Practice 26
12. The Plan of Salvation: Black Ice 28
13. Contentment: Tummy Ache 30
14. Peer Pressure: Double Dare 32
15. Humility: Last, But Not Least 34
16. Greater Love: Field Trip 36
17. Charity: Secret Generosity 38
18. Honesty: A New Doll 40
19. Stewardship: Living Sacrifices 42
20. Judging Others: KIWI 44
21. The Circle of Life: The Real Story 46
Conclusion 48

The Golden Rule

Five-Dollar Bill

"Darryl, did I ever tell you about the 'Golden Rule'?" asked Dad one afternoon.

"I've heard about the goose who laid golden eggs, but I don't know about the Golden Rule," answered Darryl.

"When I was about ten years old, an old man told me and my friends about the Golden Rule. I didn't know it was in the Bible when I first heard it. Jesus gave the Golden rule when He said, *Do unto others as you would have others do unto you.*" Dad paused for a moment. "Or in other words, treat people the way you would like them to treat you."

"Oh…can you give me an example?" asked Darryl.

"Hmmmm…Let's say you were walking along with your hands in your pockets. As you pulled your hand out to wave to your friend, the five-dollar bill in your pocket falls to the ground. You didn't notice that you dropped your money, but a person nearby noticed. What would you like that person to do for you?"

"That's easy! I want him to tell me I dropped my money."

"Exactly, you want him to be honest and kind to you. You want him to tell you that you dropped your money, rather than pick it up for himself. That's how you want to be treated. The Golden Rule says if you want to be treated kindly, then you should treat others kindly. If you saw someone drop money, you should tell him or her. Do you get it?"

"Yes!" answered Darryl.

"The Golden Rule applies in all areas of life. If you want to be treated fairly, kindly, generously, and with honesty and respect, then you should always treat others that way."

"Amen, Dad"

"Amen, Darryl."

MORAL: Respect yourself and others.

    Matthew 7:12

REFLECTIVE QUESTIONS:

    1. Why do you believe Jesus wants only the best for you?

    2. Why is it important for us to want the best for others?

Obedience

Stop! In the Name of Love

"Sidney, are you finished helping Dad wash the car?" asked Mom.

"Well, I think so. Yeah, I don't want to do that anymore," replied Sidney.

"Okay, if you are done, you can come over and help me plant the last of the flowers if you like. Just don't go out into the street. You need to stay in the driveway with your dad or come over here in the yard to play where I am."

"Okaaay" replied Sidney as she rolled her eyes.

A few minutes later Mom looked up to see where Sidney was. "Sidney," she called, "Why are you standing at the edge of the driveway? Remember that you should not go out into the street. You must play in the yard or the driveway where it is safe."

"Sidney, are you listening to your mother?" called Dad from the other side of the car. "I'm watching you carefully. You seem to be tempted. Come back up the driveway to play."

"Sidney, STOP!!! Don't run out into the street! A car is coming. Listen to me! STOP!"

That evening Mom sat down next to Sidney on the sofa. She put her arm around her and asked, "Would you like to talk?"

"I guess so, Mom."

"I know that you are not very happy right now, however discipline and consequences are necessary when you are intentionally disobedient. Learning to be obedient requires that you listen and do what is requested of you and not the opposite. I asked you to stop and not run out into the street because I love you and do not want you to get hurt. However, you did not listen and went into the street with a car coming. Dad and I want you to learn to follow the rules which are created to keep you safe."

Sidney hung her head. "I know."

"You know we can avoid consequences that we really don't like if we learn to be obedient. Do you think you can work on that? All of us will help you because we love you. Now give me a hug. I need one and I think you do also!"

"Thanks, Mom!"

"I love you, Sidney."

"I love you, too, Mom! I'm sorry I didn't listen earlier."

MORAL: The key to obedience is diligent listening and then acting upon what is heard.

Colossians 3:20; John 14:23-24

REFLECTIVE QUESTIONS:

1. Why do you believe there are consequences as a result of disobedience?

2. The Bible encourages children to obey their parents. Why do you think this is written for us in the Bible?

Gratitude

The Thankful Turkey

Once upon a time, three turkeys cleaned their rooms. Mom Turkey decided to give them each a quarter for working so hard. The three turkeys asked to go to the store to buy candy, but mom turkey made them go one at a time since they usually got in trouble together.

Caleb, the first turkey, took his quarter and started walking to the store. It was a very blustery day. Just as he stepped over the gutter, Wooooosh! The wind blew, and he dropped his quarter down in the gutter.

Now Mr. Mouse lives down in the gutter. When Caleb saw Mr. Mouse, he asked, "Would you bring me my quarter?"

Mr. Mouse, being the nice mouse that he is, carried the quarter out of the gutter and gave it to the first turkey. The first turkey continued on to the store and bought his candy.

Soon Cameron, the second turkey, was walking along to the store. Just as she stepped over the gutter, Woooosh! The wind blew, and she dropped her quarter down in the gutter.

Now Mr. Mouse lives down in the gutter. When Cameron saw Mr. Mouse, she asked, "Would you bring me my quarter?"

Mr. Mouse, being the nice mouse that he is, carried the quarter out of the gutter and gave it to the second turkey. The second turkey continued on to the store and bought her candy.

Now it was time for Mason, the third turkey, to go to the store. Just as he stepped over the gutter, Woooosh! The wind blew, and just like the other two turkeys, he dropped his quarter down in the gutter.

When Mason saw Mr. Mouse, he asked, "Would you please bring me my quarter? Please, please?!? I really want some candy. Would you please bring me my quarter?"

After Mr. Mouse carried the quarter out of the gutter, the third turkey yelled with excitement, "Thank you! Thank you, Mr. Mouse! You didn't have to do that for me. I really appreciate your help."

"You know, Mason," said Mr. Mouse, "There were two other *turkeys* that came this way, and neither of them said 'thank you' or 'please.' I want you to know that a lot of people have dropped money down in this gutter over the years. Because you said 'thank you,' I'm going to go down and get as much money as I can and give it to you."

Soon Mason was on his way to the store with lots of money to buy lots of candy.

MORAL: It pays to show gratitude.

Luke 17:11-19

REFLECTIVE QUESTIONS:

1. Why is it important to acknowledge the kindness of others?

2. How would Jesus have us respond when acts of kindness are shown to us?

Forgiveness

I Forgot

When Mason and his two turkey siblings returned from the store with candy, Mason had a lot more than the others.

"How did you get so much more than the others, Mason?" asked Mom Turkey.

"Mr. Mouse gave me lots of money," Mason responded. "After I dropped my quarter down in the gutter, he brought it up for me. Because I said 'thank you,' he gave me extra money for having good manners."

"That was very nice of Mr. Mouse," said Mom. "I will thank him next time I see him."

"Hey, I dropped my quarter down in the gutter, too," pouted Caleb.

"I did too!" whined Cameron.

"But we forgot to say 'thank you,'" they cried together.

Caleb tried to explain, "I was so happy to get the quarter back…I just forgot, Mom. Man, I wish I had known. I could have gotten more money."

"That would not be a good reason to be polite, Caleb. You should be polite even if no money is involved," said Mom.

"I knooow…I knoooow."

A few hours later, Caleb was still mad at himself for not saying "thank you" to Mr. Mouse for his kind deed. He was also mad because he was all out of candy.

"What's the matter with you, Caleb?" asked Mom.

"I'm still mad at myself for being rude to Mr. Mouse."

"Oh, I see. We all forget or make mistakes sometimes. You're not a bad person. Forgive yourself and try again. God still loves you. God is able to forgive our sins and bad memories."

"How do I try again?" asked Caleb.

"You know where Mr. Mouse lives. You and your sister should stop by to apologize. He is a forgiving mouse. One rule applies…don't take any extra money if he offers. Earn it the right way."

MORAL: Forgive yourself, God does.

Philippians 3:12-14; Romans 3:23-24

REFLECTIVE QUESTIONS:

1. Why do you believe it is better for Caleb to let go of the mistake he made?

2. How has God shown His love for us in the form of forgiveness?

Hospitality

Sleepover

Junior and Simon were quite excited about the planned sleepover and pizza night. This was going to be an exciting adventure for them both.

"Do we have any more pizza, Mom?" yelled Junior up the stairs.

"Just one slice," replied mom.

"Oh, you can have the last piece, Simon. I'm stuffed anyways.

"Mom, Simon is on his way up for the last slice!"

"Thanks, buddy…I think I have room for one more slice," grinned Simon.

"So, how was the movie, guys?" asked Mom as she came down to join the boys for a few minutes before going off to bed.

"It was pretty good, Mom. Nice guys do finish first when they have faith," replied Junior.

"Speaking of first, which one of you is hopping into the shower first?" asked Mom. "It will help you sleep better."

"Do you want to go first, Simon?" Junior asked.

"Sure, I'll get it over with," replied Simon.

Two hours later, the noise of the boys playing woke Mom up. She had dozed off.

"Okay, boys, time for bed!" she yelled down the stairs. "Lights out!"

"Which bunk bed do you sleep in? Top or bottom?"

"Well, I sleep on the bottom most of the time," replied Junior. "What about you?"

"I like the top bunk, but after I rolled over and fell on the floor, my mom said I had to sleep on the bottom bunk. As long as you don't tell her, I can sleep on the top bunk tonight so you can have the bottom as always."

"Ooooh no," Junior said. "I'm not getting in the middle of your family feud. You can have the bottom. I'll sleep up top tonight."

"Thanks for keeping me on the straight and narrow, Junior, and for this great party!"

MORAL: Practice good hospitality to all.

   Genesis 18: 3-5

REFLECTIVE QUESTIONS:

   1. Jesus encourages us to practice hospitality. How was Junior hospitable to Simon?

   2. Why is it important to help your friends not to compromise what they are taught?

Thriftiness

Grab Bag

"Lauren, I need to go to the mall today to pick up something," said Mom. "I don't have any extra spending money, so you need to take a couple of dollars of your own money if you want to buy a grab bag at your favorite store."

"Okay, Mom!" Lauren replied as she ran to her room to get some money out of her piggy bank.

A little while later, as they entered the mall, Mom said, "We're going to go to my store first, Lauren, so I can buy what we came to the mall for. Then we will stop and let you select a grab bag."

"Okay!" Lauren sighed with contentment. She didn't mind going with her mom first because she knew she would get to go to her store, too.

After Mom bought her things, they walked to Lauren's favorite store.

"Lauren, do you have your money?" asked Mom.

"Yes, Mom," Lauren replied as she patted her pocket.

They spent a few minutes looking at the various games and toys in the aisles, and then Mom suggested that they go to the counter to pick out a grab bag. Much to Lauren's amazement, she was allowed to select two grab bags because they were two for the price of one that day!

"Mom, can you believe it? I got two bags! Two!" Lauren jumped up and down with excitement as she paid the cashier.

"Mom…"

"Yes, dear?" asked Mom.

"Dad is going to be maaaad at me!"

"Why would he be mad?"

"Because I'm not supposed to spend my money at the mall. I'm supposed to spend MY money at the BANK!"

"It will be okay, Lauren," laughed Mom. "Dad will be happy with what you bought today, especially because you got two for the price of one. And, I'm glad to know that you listen to your father. He wants you to understand the importance of saving."

MORAL: It is important to practice careful spending and saving.

Luke 16:10-12

REFLECTIVE QUESTIONS:

1. Why do you believe it is important not to be wasteful with your money?

2. Why do you believe that Jesus will trust you with more when you manage your money well?

Teamwork

1, 2, 3 Lift!

"It's time for spring clean-up, everybody!" declared Mom. "Tomorrow morning I want all three of you to fill this box with clothes and shoes that are too small for you. We will take it to the homeless shelter tomorrow afternoon."

The next day, everyone found items to put in the box. Russ had shirts and pants, Derek had a few pair of shoes, and Dana had lots of everything. The box was full. When Dana tried to lift the box, she could not because it was too heavy. Derek and Russ each tried, but they couldn't lift it either.

"Mom," the crew shouted. "We have a problem."

"I'm listening," said Mom.

"We've all tried, but nobody can lift this box of clothing. It's too heavy."

Mom looked at her three children standing around the box.

"See if you can lift it, Mom," encouraged Dana. "You're stronger than us."

"Thanks for the compliment, Dana, but you three need to learn how to work together."

"How?" they asked with puzzled looks on their faces.

"Haven't you heard of teamwork?" When no one answered, Mom asked, "Have you tried to lift the box together instead of by yourselves?"

The three children shook their heads "no."

"Okay, try putting all of your muscles together to lift the box."

After a little coordinating, Russ took one side of the box, while Dana and Derek grabbed the other sides.

"1, 2, 3 lift!" said Russ.

Much to their surprise, the box came off the ground! They carried it to the garage and put it in the truck.

Mom smiled and said, "Mission accomplished, kids!"

MORAL: Six hands are better than two.

Luke 5:17-26

REFLECTIVE QUESTIONS:

1. In what ways have you been able to accomplish more when working with others as a team?

2. Why do you believe Jesus encourages us to work together and pray together?

20.

Simplicity

Game Rules

"What are you reading, Son?" asked Dad.

"I have an earth science test tomorrow," Collin responded. "I'm trying to remember the difference between hibernation and migration. Bears hibernate and birds migrate?"

"Yes. That reminds me of one of my favorite sayings, 'I believe birds fly south in the winter because it's cold. If I were a bird, I'd fly south, too.'"

"So when it gets cold, birds fly south?" asked Collin.

"Yes, it's that simple. When it starts to get cold, birds must fly to a warmer area.

God made all creatures great and small. As we try to understand the creatures, we sometimes put big labels and big words on things. We can also complicate our lives by worldly wisdom."

"I'm not following you…what are you talking about?"

"Sorry, son, another one of my sermons, I guess. What I'm trying to say is life can be more peaceful if we keep things plain and simple. Remember the other night when we were playing a game with Raquel? Your sister kept adding new rules. After a while we had so many rules that the game was no longer fun."

"Hey yeah, that's right! She made the game too hard."

"People make life too hard by adding too many rules, too many big words, and too many tricks. All of the laws of the prophets and all ten of the commandments were summarized in one big sentence: *Love the Lord your God with all your heart, all your soul, all your strength and all your mind, and Love your neighbor as yourself…do this and you will live.* That's what Jesus said in Luke 10:27-28."

"Love God and love your neighbor?"

"Yes, and you shall live, son," smiled Dad. "I hope you pass your science test."

"I will, Dad, but I need a nap right now. I think I'll go to my room and hibernate for a while."

MORAL: Keep it simple.

Luke 10:27-28; Galatians 5:13-15

REFLECTIVE QUESTIONS:

1. What is the greatest command given to us by God?

2. How does making things easier to accomplish help you complete a task?

Doing a Good Job

The Paper Route

Cass decided to spend an afternoon with his cousin Eric who just started his first job as a paper carrier. On the front of Eric's bicycle was a large basket that Eric filled with newspapers. He also loaded his sack with papers and carried it across his shoulder.

"So, Eric, why did you get a job? Wouldn't you rather be playing?" asked Cass as they started towards the first house.

"Well, I need the money. I do a lot of things at school, and my paper route money pays for some of my sports stuff, class projects, and field trips," answered Eric. "Plus I can buy ice cream or a new video game if I wanted."

Earlier Cass had asked what he could do to help, and Eric had decided to let him throw the papers.

Suddenly Eric hollered, "Cass! What are you doing? Mrs. Moody will never find her paper behind the mulberry bush!!!"

"I'm sorry. I'll get it. I didn't think it was that big of a deal where the paper landed. It just has to be in the yard." Cass crawled behind Mrs. Moody's mulberry bush, found the newspaper, and tossed it on the front porch.

"Well, when the time comes for me to collect the newspaper money, I have to go to everyone's door. If a customer doesn't find her newspaper, she isn't going to pay me for it and will tell me I didn't deliver it. But my boss makes me pay for those papers out of my paycheck, so I lose money."

Eric understood that he had a choice about how he was going to deliver the papers every evening. He could sling the papers so they landed on the doorsteps, or he could throw them behind the bushes and not care if a customer ever found the paper.

Eric knew that how diligent he was in delivering the papers reflected on him and on the money he received, not on the customer or the newspaper company. He also knew that if he set out to do the job right, the outcome would always be pleasing.

For, God is pleased with our work when we put our heart into it.

MORAL: Our work is pleasing when we put our heart into it.

Colossians 3:23-24

REFLECTIVE QUESTIONS:

1. In all that we do, whom do you believe we should seek to please?

2. How did Eric demonstrate that he was a good friend to Cass?

Prayer

Straight Paths

"Mom, tell me again…what exactly is prayer?" asked Ronnie.

"Prayer is talking and listening to God. Through prayer we ask God for help, for guidance in doing His will, or just tell God how much we love Him. Let's look at something in the Bible to help you understand." Mom picked up her Bible and flipped through the pages. "Here it is. Proverbs 3:5 reads:

Trust in the Lord with all your heart and lean not on your own understanding; in all your ways acknowledge him, and he will make your paths straight.

Prayer is a way to include God in our lives in every way. Through prayer we trust God and remember how much we need him. We ask God to direct our paths and to help us live and make decisions that will please Him. God answers our prayers by giving us wisdom and power to do the right thing. Do you understand, Ronnie?"

"Yes."

"Jesus prayed for strength when he was feeling weak at Gethsemane just before going to the cross. God helped by giving Jesus strength to lay down His life for us. Jesus also taught us the Lord's Prayer. Have you memorized it yet?"

"Yes. We learned it at church. It starts with *Our Father in heaven*."

"Good! Whenever you have questions, just ask! We can talk about what the Lord's Prayer means, too."

"Thanks, Mom!"

"You're welcome. I'm here for you anytime."

MORAL: Pray without ceasing.

    Matthew 26:36-46

REFLECTIVE QUESTIONS:

1. What are some of the reasons why we should pray?

2. So, how do we make sure that the path we walk each day is the way God wants us to go?

Diligence

Practice, Practice, Practice

"Practice. Practice. Practice, Stephen. That's what my math teacher told me when I was in school," said Dad. "She told us if we wanted to do well on the test, we had to practice doing the math problems. If we didn't understand, we could ask questions. The more you practice, the easier the test will be."

"I hear you, Dad, but math can be sooo confusing," complained Stephen.

"I know, but keep paying attention in class, keep doing your best on your homework, and ask questions when you don't understand. If you do those three things all the time, you will not fail. I am confident of that."

"What makes you so confident, Dad? I'm not so confident."

"Experience, Son, I've tried it that way, and it worked for me. Anything we want to do well requires practice or hard work. Musicians have to practice their music. Athletes have to practice and exercise to be good at their sports. Farmers have to learn and practice being good farmers. And Christians have to learn and put into practice the words of Christ. It takes time. It takes effort. It's something that won't happen if we are too lazy."

"I hear ya, Dad. I'll try practicing these math problems some more."

"Good, now, tell me where you're stuck…maybe I can help you."

MORAL: Diligence is a must.

Proverbs 10:4; Hebrews 6:10-12

REFLECTIVE QUESTIONS:

1. In what ways does practicing help you to become better?

2. Why do you believe it is important to never give up?

The Plan of Salvation

Black Ice

"I'm sorry kids; we can't go out to the movies. The weatherman says there's a lot of freezing rain coming down outside. Freezing rain often causes black ice. It's just too dangerous to drive today."

"I've never seen black ice before. What does it look like, Dad?" asked Martin.

"When a thin layer of ice covers the road, we call it 'black ice.' The ice is clear so it looks black, just like the color of the road. Drivers have a hard time seeing it, and it's very slippery. Sometimes driving on the ice causes the car to slide."

"That could be fun! Like a sleigh ride!" giggled Danielle.

"I don't think so, Danielle," said Dad. "I've been told that black ice causes the worst kind of road conditions. Drivers shouldn't go out unless they have to because if the car slides on black ice, it does what it wants to. The driver loses control and can have an accident."

"How do you get rid of black ice?" asked Martin. "I want to get out of this house…it's been snowing for two days!"

"Well, the ice either melts away from the heat of the sun, or the city workers make the road better by putting salt on the road."

"What does salt do?" everyone asked together.

"Salt helps the car tires grip the ice. It makes the ice a little bumpy so that it's not so slick. I think salt might help with the melting too, but I'm not sure."

"So, Dad, salt and sun helps get rid of black ice?" asked Martin. Dad nodded his head.

"If only we had some salt and sun," said Danielle as she looked out the window, "We could go to the movies."

"Yes. You know, that reminds me that the Bible teaches the same things. The Son of God, Jesus, melts our sins away if we believe and invite His warmth and forgiveness into our hearts. Also, with the help of God's Spirit, we can become the salt of the earth. We can help make the world a better place by helping people get rid of the black ice or sin in their lives. Does that make sense to you guys?"

"Uh, say that again, Dad, but a little slower this time. I think I understand but maybe you can explain it," said Danielle.

MORAL: Jesus saves us from sin (we can help)

John 3:16-17

REFLECTIVE QUESTIONS:

1. In what ways can we invite Jesus into our hearts?

2. How can we become like salt and season the world to help make things better?

Contentment

Tummy Ache

"Ooooh. Aaaah. Oh man. I have a tummy ache, Dad," moaned Marc.

"So how did that happen?" asked Dad.

"Well, I ate two hotdogs, chips, a pickle, and three scoops of ice cream at Kyan's house.

"Oh, that's quite a bit. Last I checked, you could only eat one hotdog," said Dad.

"Well, Mom only gives me one." "Did I ever tell you that Mother knows best? And three scoops of ice cream? That sounds like a bit much, Marc," said Dad.

"Kyan was eating three, so I thought I'd join him."

"Kyan is two years older than you are. His stomach can handle more than yours can. I think its time for a lesson in contentment."

"Contend what?" asked Marc.

"I said contentment. Con-tent-ment. It means knowing and being satisfied with your limits. It can also mean being at peace with yourself when you've done the best that you can in a race and you're not worried about winning or losing. People, who are content with life, don't overdo things. When they are full, they stop eating. When they have reached a certain limit, they stop spending money. And when they have run as far as they can, they stop to rest. Is all of this making any sense?"

"I think so, Dad,…but I'm only a kid. How can I resist ice cream?"

"You don't have to resist it. You just have to resist eating too much. It's not easy, Marc. I have trouble with contentment too," said Dad. "I spend too much money at the bookstore sometimes. I forget that I can only read one book at a time. Too many books means not enough gas to drive you to football practice or for me to drive to work."

"That's not good, Dad."

MORAL: Contentment brings peace to the soul (and the stomach).

1 Timothy 6:6

REFLECTIVE QUESTIONS:

1. How do you believe that contentment brings peace?

2. Why is it important to follow your heart and not the actions of others?

Peer Pressure

Double Dare

"Mom, what's a dare?" asked Cory.

"It's like a challenge. Someone may dare you or challenge you to see if you will respond to what he says by doing or saying what the challenge calls for."

"Why do you ask?" inquired Mom.

"Well, Trey, one of the boys in my class, is always daring someone to do different things and makes fun of the person when he doesn't want to."

"Has he ever dared you to do something that you did not want to do?" asked Mom. "Well, yes, it happened today. He really made fun of me and actually 'double dared' me to take a piece of candy out of the candy jar on the teacher's desk."

"Where was your teacher?"

"In the cafeteria. She asked me to go back to the classroom with Trey because he forgot his lunch. Trey told me on the way back that he did not really forget his lunch. He had left it in the classroom on purpose so that he would be able to go back to get candy."

Cory paused and then continued, "Mom, we are only allowed to have a treat when the teacher gives it to us. And one of the rules is we are not allowed to go into our teacher's space unless we are invited. I guess that's why it was a double dare - one dare to go into her space without permission and the second dare to take a piece of candy without permission."

"Hmmm," said Mom. "Would you like to share with me how you responded to this double dare?"

"Well, I was thinking about how much Trey teases the other kids, and I really did not want him to do that to me. But I was also thinking about how disappointed my teacher would be. I would break two rules if I did what Trey asked. I knew that would not be right, so I turned around and just did not respond to Trey's dare."

"How do you feel about your decision?" inquired Mom.

"I feel good about it now that it's over, but Trey was not nice to me as we walked back to the lunchroom. But that was okay, too; I just walked really fast to get back to my other friends. I know I am not supposed to break rules, Mom, I'm supposed to keep them."

"That's right, Cory," said Mom, "And remember to never let others determine your response in any situation. Always respond in a manner that you know is best and one that is pleasing to God."

MORAL: Never let the actions of others determine your actions, reaction or response.

Ephesians 4:14

REFLECTIVE QUESTIONS:

1. How do you think you would respond to Trey's suggestion?

2. Why is it important to read your Bible so that you will know how Jesus would want you to respond to Trey?

Humility

Last, But Not Least

"How was school today, Reggie?" asked Dad as Reggie dropped his books on the kitchen table.

"Not bad! Actually a good thing happened. My teacher put me in the front of the lunch line because I was not fighting like most of the other kids were. They were going crazy! You should have heard them, Dad. 'I want to be first today! You were first yesterday! I'm going to be first! No, I'm going first!' It was crazy."

"Why didn't you join in the fight? Didn't you want to be first, too?"

"It doesn't matter that much to me, Dad. I don't mind if others go before me. I'll eat at some point."

"That's very wise of you. A lot of kids don't see it that way," replied Dad.

"Don't get me wrong. I don't mind being first, especially when I'm hungry, but I just don't want to fight about it."

"Well, I think your teacher made a wise decision. She was probably trying to teach everyone something Jesus taught us. He said, *Those who exalt themselves will be humbled, but those who humble themselves will be exalted.* You were put at the front of the line because you were demonstrating humility by not fighting and being willing to get in line anywhere. Those who were fighting were trying to exalt themselves. I'm proud of you, Reggie. Keep it up!"

MORAL: Trust God to take care of you.

Matthew 23:12; Luke 14:7-11, 18:9-14

REFLECTIVE QUESTIONS:

1. Who would you rather make the decision to place you at the front of the line?

2. What type of responsibility is required of you when selected to lead the line?

Greater Love

Field Trip

Mrs. Riley's class was preparing for their big field trip of the year to the beach. Many of the students had never been to the beach, so there was much excitement in the air.

"Ben and Bennett!" Mrs. Riley alarmingly called out. "You two have been struggling with your behavior by acting inappropriately towards each other for the past few days. I've given each of you every indication that if you are not able to behave accordingly in the classroom, how could I expect that you will behave properly on the field trip for the museum guides and chaperones? You will not be able to join us on the field trip."

"No, Mrs. Riley! No, please, please let us go!" the two boys pleaded.

"We'll be good! We'll be good!" promised Bennett.

"Boys, you have not proven that to me nor to your classmates. That's the end of this discussion for now."

As the class went out for recess, Alex lingered around Mrs. Riley.

"Alex, what is it? What's on your mind?" asked Mrs. Riley.

"Mrs. Riley," Alex replied, "Ben and Bennett are my friends, and if they cannot go on the trip, I cannot go either. In fact, I will take their punishment for them. I've been to the beach before and want to stay here so that they can go. That's what I want to do, Mrs. Riley."

"Well, Alex, that is a very noble thing for you to consider doing. You are a true friend, and I'm proud of you."

Now, of course, Ben and Bennett understood that there are consequences when we break the rules. Alex understood, however, he was willing to suffer the consequences on behalf of his friends, because he truly cared for them and wanted them to be happy. He was not concerned about himself, a selfless act and a true friend indeed.

MORAL: Christ Himself teaches us the true meaning of friendship.

John 15:13

REFLECTIVE QUESTIONS:

1. How did Jesus demonstrate His love for us?

2. How did Alex demonstrate his love for his friends?

Charity

Secret Generosity

"Dad, can I have more money for lunch?" asked Conner. "I'm a little short."

"I gave you enough for the whole week plus your allowance. What happened?" asked Dad.

"My friend Andrew didn't have enough money to buy his lunch yesterday. I slid him a dollar while no one was watching. I didn't want him to be embarrassed by not having enough money."

"Wow! You sound more like a Christian every day," Dad said with excitement while handing Conner two dollars.

"I only need one dollar, Dad."

"You get one plus a bonus for being generous."

"Thanks, Dad!"

"Conner, did I tell you that there are at least thirty scriptures in the Bible that encourage us to give?" asked Dad.

"I gotta go to school, but you can tell me about them later."

"Alright! Have a good day…I'm proud of you! See you."

MORAL: It is in giving that we receive.

Matthew 6:1-4; Luke 6:38

REFLECTIVE QUESTIONS:

1. How did Conner's act of giving turn out to be a blessing for him?

2. Why do you believe Conner's father was proud of him?

Honesty

A New Doll

Jessica and Mom went to the mall one morning so Mom could buy a new dress for a very special occasion that she and Dad planned to attend. When they got home, Jessica carried some of her dolls to Mom's bedroom and sat on the floor. She watched as Mom admired her new dress in the long mirror.

"Mom?"

"Yes, Dear?"

"May I have a new doll?"

"No, Jessica, you may not have a new doll."

"Well, how come?"

"Because we do not have ANY money to purchase a new doll."

"But, Mom, if we don't have ANY money, how come you just bought a new dress at the mall?"

Mom turned away from the mirror and knelt beside Jessica. "I'm sorry, Jessica. My response was not honest. The real reason you may not have a new doll is because you don't need another doll. You already have enough dolls to play with."

"Oh, okay!" Jessica picked up her dolls and went back to playing.

MORAL: Honesty is the best policy.

    Proverbs 12:22

REFLECTIVE QUESTIONS:

1. At what point was Jessica able to accept that she could not have a new doll?

2. Why do you believe that being honest is the right thing to do?

Stewardship

Living Sacrifices

"How was Sunday school today, Claire?" asked Mom.

"Not bad. Our lesson was about stewardship. We learned how to manage wisely the resources that God gives us."

"Resources?" responded Mom. "That's a big word for fourth graders. What did your teacher mean by resources?"

"She meant our time, talent, strength and money," said Claire.

"Oh, that's good. What did she say about money?"

"Mom, is this a test? I was paying attention today. Miss Lassiter encouraged us to tithe 10 percent. That's what the Bible teaches. She said if our allowance is $5.00 then we should give God at least 50 cents. If we do, God said He would bless us with more."

"That's right," replied Mom. "God wants us to give freely. Sometimes people give more than 10 percent. Let's see if you understood what Miss Lassiter was saying. Do we only give God 10 percent of our time, talent or strength?"

"No, Mom, time, talent and strength are a little different. We're supposed to give God much more than 10 percent. Romans 12:1-2 says we should be living sacrifices in response to God's love and mercy towards us. In response to God's love, we should serve in His Kingdom and not live like the world does."

"Wow! Claire, I'm impressed" said Mom with a smile on her face. "You really were paying attention. I'm so proud of you."

"It's the least I can do. Not bad for a fourth grader, huh?"

MORAL: Love God back.

Proverbs 3:9-10; Romans 12:1-2

REFLECTIVE QUESTIONS:

1. What are some the ways you can love God back?

2. How can you manage what you have wisely?

Judging Others

Kiwi

One day Parker went to the market with Mom. She asked him if he wanted to try a kiwi instead of an orange in his school lunch. Parker looked at the strange, brownish-green, fuzzy fruit and responded, "That's funny looking. I don't think I like kiwi."

"Parker, have you ever tried kiwi?" asked his mother.

"No, Mom, but I can tell by the looks of things that I don't like it."

Later that evening, Parker's mother found herself pondering her son's response to the kiwi. She was bothered a little bit because he was not willing to try the kiwi. But, she was bothered even more by his reason – he didn't like the way it looked. She hoped Parker would learn to make decisions based on knowledge, not on outward appearances. She knew that judging on outward appearances was not good, especially with people.

Mom decided to have a talk with Parker about kiwi and life. But first, she returned to the store to buy some kiwi.

"Parker," Mom called, "Come here…I'd like you to try something."

"What's this?" asked Parker.

"Kiwi, please try a piece. It's the fruit I wanted you to try yesterday," responded Mom.

"Okay, Mom, but just a small piece. You know I don't like this stuff." After a small bite, Parker was pleasantly surprised by the taste. "Wow, it's not bad. Let me try another piece."

"I'm glad you like it, Parker. I was hoping you would…you can have it all," said Mom as she gave him the rest of the fruit. "I want to share some things with you about kiwi and life. Sometimes we treat each other like kiwi. We look at each other from the outside and then decide that we don't like each other. Those decisions may be unfair and incorrect. Parker, I'd like you to practice getting to know others and fruit before deciding that you don't like them. Do you understand what I'm saying?"

"I understand, Mom," Parker responded. "I'd miss out on a lot of good fruit and good people if I decided not to like them because of how they look on the outside."

"That's the spirit, Parker,…that's the Holy Spirit. I think that way of learning about life and people will be pleasing to God."

MORAL: Quick judgments can cause big mistakes.

Luke 6:37; 1 Peter 1:22-23; 1 Samuel 16:7

REFLECTIVE QUESTIONS:

1. Why do you believe it is important not to judge something you have not experienced?

2. Why do you believe it's more important to get to know the heart of a person and not just how they look?

The Circle of Life

The Real Story

"Dad, your hair is really getting gray," Anthony pointed out.

"I told you that it's the hair spray that I use," grinned Dad. "The hair spray colors my hair. It makes it look gray. I'm too young to have gray hair."

"Sure, Dad! So tell me again why the hair spray doesn't color my hair gray?"

"That's my story and I'm sticking with it," said Dad.

"What's the real story?"

"It's the story about the circle of life I suppose. I was out for a run the other day and I was looking at the beautiful golden leaves on the trees. I compared it to my hair. Just like the leaves on the trees turn from green to golden in autumn, my hair turns from black to gray as I get older. Everything grows old and dies, but we have the gift of eternal life in heaven if we believe in God's promises."

"Everything dies?"

"Every living thing on earth - the birds and the bees and the apples in the trees…and lions and tigers and bears, oh my!"

"I've heard that somewhere" observed Anthony.

"There is a burst of new life in the spring, but even the vegetables that the farmers grow in the field grow old and die if we don't pick them and eat them first."

"But in Christ we can live again?" asked Anthony.

"Yes, if we believe in our Savior Jesus Christ, we will live forever with Him after our life on earth is completed."

"Sounds good to me, Dad."

"Me too, Anthony. So, when people start to turn gray, it's okay. They are just getting ready for heaven."

MORAL: The circle of life is real.

John 1:10-12; John 3:16

REFLECTIVE QUESTIONS:

1. How does the end of one season bring the beginning of a new one?

2. How does it feel to know that you can live life forever with Jesus?

Conclusion

Trust in the Lord with all of your heart and lean not on your own understanding; in all your ways submit to him, and he will make your paths straight. Do not be wise in your own eyes; fear the Lord and shun evil. This will bring health to your body and nourishment to your bones.

Honor the Lord with your wealth, with the first fruits of all your crops; then your barns will be filled to overflowing, and your vats will brim over with new wine.

My son, do not despise the Lord's discipline and do not resent his rebuke, because the Lord disciplines those he loves, as a father the son he delights in.

Blessed is the man that finds wisdom, the man who gains understanding for she is more profitable than silver and yields better returns than gold. She is more precious than rubies; nothing you desire can compare with her. Long life is in her right hand; in her left hand are riches and honor. Her ways are pleasant ways, and all her paths are peace. She is a tree of life to those who embrace her; those who hold of her fast will be blessed.

Proverbs 3:5-18